THE MAN WHO STANDS IN LINE

THE

MAN

WHO

STANDS

IN

LINE

A Collection of Very Short Works

by

Kenneth M Halpern

εpsilon Books

ISBN: 1-945671-00-9

ISBN-13: 978-1-945671-00-5

Library of Congress Control Number: 2017911508

Published by Epsilon Books

Printed in the United States of America

"Charge" first appeared in Caveat Lector, Volume XXI, Issue 1, 2010

Cover Art by Richie Montgomery

Cover Layout by Sara Zieve Miller

First Edition

CONTENTS

The Man Who Stands In Line

I stand in line, waiting.
Many others stand ahead of me, waiting.
Occasionally, the line moves.

I have spent most of my life in line.
My son will spend most of his.
I do not complain.
It is the way of the world.

People walk by.
Where are they going?
They are too busy to wait in line.
I wonder how they make do.
If they try to cheat,
they will get in trouble.
I respect the rules.

Once, I tried to cut the line.
I tried to bargain, bribe.
They sent me to the back.
There are other lines.
Short lines. Fast lines.
They said I must wait in this one.

Today I can see the front.
Others pour in from all sides.
How can so many do this?
I ask one as he passes.
He shoots me a knowing smile.
My line moves so slowly.
How many really are in it?

When I first arrived,
I was unsure which line
to stand in.

They told me this one,
without having asked why.
I tried to explain.
This one, they barked.

Finally, it is my turn.
I proudly step forward.
A man asks what I want.
I am frightened, hopeful.
How does one answer this?

I begin to speak.
He cuts me off.
You are in the wrong line.
Next.

Beware the Fly

When you are at home in the ordinary chaos of things coming and going, it is easy to ignore a fly. This can be a mistake.

There are flies, and there are flies. Pay close attention to the shape of the wings, the striations, the abdominal patina. These may be the give-away, the sign that this fly, out of billions, is a killer. It is the anathema, the 1943 copper penny, the brown recluse.

This does not mean it necessarily will go out of its way to kill you. It may be busy or lazy or simply not in the mood. It may bide its time until your child is asleep or it may decide you altogether unworthy of the effort. Then again, it may not.

You won't know you are dead until some time has passed. This fly looks almost identical to any other and seems innocuous. Perhaps if you hadn't shooed it or tried to swat it or made eye contact or failed to offer it a lucrative compensation package it simply would have gone away. But it did not, and the fault probably is yours.

Of course, you may not have recognized the fly, thought it ordinary, harmless. That is no excuse. If anything, it is insulting.

There are 230 visual characteristics that can be used to identify a fly. Killer and ordinary flies differ in only one of these, and nobody is sure which. Even the most renowned expert has little chance of telling.

But perhaps you can do better, since you care, since you're the one who will die.

There's no certainty, only statistics. Find a way to bend these in your favor and perhaps you will live another day. Avoid the fly, run from it. Sometimes ignoring it can help; if there is no such thing it cannot hurt you.

Why should there be this fly? It has no right to exist, to threaten you and your child! But it does, and if you encounter it perhaps you can seduce it, persuade it to find somebody else – somebody less important, somebody less you (or your child). This rarely works, or perhaps you *are* that somebody else.

The sad truth remains: the fly is out there, unrelenting, buzzing, waiting. You must accept that it will kill you. If it is indeed a killer. Does it want your death or just some sugar?

Once the fly has bitten you, you will die. The fatality rate is 100%. Sometimes it is quick and painless, other times it can last for decades, culminating in one of many lingering, debilitating conditions. The symptoms are indistinguishable from ordinary illness, it is probably best not to bother with a doctor.

Save your money for a quality tomb. Finding a good place to spend eternity is difficult. Do you think there is room left in heaven or hell? Real estate is in high demand, you'll likely end up stuck in your grave. Be certain it's a nice one. Most important, make sure there are no holes, or a fly may get in.

Charge

Resemble me,
　but not too closely,
　　or you will appear to mock me,
　　and not too faintly,
　　　or you will show disdain for me.
　　　Flatter me,
　　　　but not too strongly,
　　　　　or you will disgust me,
　　　　　and not too subtly,
　　　　　　or you will displease me.
　　　　　　Beg me,
　　　　　　　but not too insistently,
　　　　　　　　or you will annoy me,
　　　　　　　　and not too quietly,
　　　　　　　　　or you will fail to move me.
　　　　　　　　Fear me,
　　　　　　　　　but not too much,
　　　　　　　　　　or you will hate me,
　　　　　　　　　　and not too little,
　　　　　　　　　　　or you will offend me.
　　　　　　　　　Obey me,
　　　　　　　　　　but not too readily,
　　　　　　　　　　　or you will repel me,
　　　　　　　　　　　and not too slowly,
　　　　　　　　　　　　or you will anger me.
　　　　　　　　　　　　Now go forth and multiply,
　　　　　　　　　　　　so many eyes
　　　　　　　　　　　　to mirror me without end.

Beyond the Bordello

Men come in and fuck me. I don't know who or what they are.

My Keeper promised they won't hurt me if I do what they want. She said they even could be nice.

Are they a type of dog? I had a dog once, but it went away. The men are bigger than me and some seem surprised to see me.

They say I should be in school. What is school? Is that where the men live?

My Keeper says I am better off here. She says men can be managed here, controlled. It is safe here.

I trust my Keeper. She has always lived here, like the ones before her. One day I hope to be just like her.

I sometimes wonder why the men come here and do this silly thing.

Tock

Tick Tock says the clock.
Tock Tick say the sick.

Turn back your hands,
they beg in vain.
They are digging your graves,
it laughs insane.

We'll smash your dial,
they threaten meekly.
I have another,
it chortles obscenely.

Tick Tock says the clock.
Nobody hears or speaks.

Prosthetic Egg

I broke my tooth and cursed. Can't a man have any peace without damned progress? Now they've gone and done it.

First they started synthesizing and amalgamating, and my food tasted like Styrofoam, plastic mcChunklets, Flopper with Cheesespliz.

Then they started sticking fake parts on us to replace the ones we lost racing fast cars or watching TV or that we just didn't feel like keeping.

I put up with steroid soaked pigs and veggies made from cardboard, but this really takes it. They've given me a prosthetic egg for breakfast.

Threshold

I departed a youth
on clouds of dream
for wherever the
wind chanced to blow.
They saw me off, friend,
lover, rival.

They saw me off,
a room full of cheer.
Hip hip hooray
for the traveler,
merry be his journey.
Hip hip hooray
for the traveler,
cheer him on his way.

Forever we will be here.
When you return,
wayward son,
come in from the cold.
Rock, tree, and earth may move
but we always will be here
to greet the weary walker.

Long and far was my journey
before I found a path home,
worn, wayward, weary.
I sought my tavern's
warm embrace.
Mustn't one hearth remain
even the forsaken?

That loyal friend
lay within sight,
home to so many
invented memories,
so much imagined mirth.
No din issued,
no inviting amber glow.

I pushed the door open,
it swung on rusty hinges,
useless guardian, silent
epitaph. Only an empty shell
remained. Where the merry
troop had gone
nobody could tell.
When asked,
a passerby shrugged.
"They closed some time ago."

Mayoral

Run, run, run for Mayor!
I want to run for Mayor!

If I am Mayor, I can decide things the way they should be decided, the way I want them decided, help the good doing good and keep the bad from doing bad.

But if I run for Mayor, I'll have to decide everything, for everyone, all the time. Meetings and boredom and arguing and convincing and negotiating and alienating and listening. Best not to run, let somebody else do the dirty work.

But if I am not Mayor, then there's a chance somebody will make a decision I don't like, would not have made. There is an other, and he is unpredictable. I do not like this other, he is not me. Something that matters to me may go awry. The good may do bad, the bad may do good. Best not to vote, or I will be responsible for this other.

Run, run, run from Mayor.
I want to stay home.

Seemly

You are unseemly.

There is no room
for unseemly things
in my world.

You do not exist
in my world.

You exist in this
world.

It is not my world,
and is unseemly.

My world must
be seemly.

If you were
to enter my world
it would become
unseemly.

I must remove you
from the unseemly
world.

Then my world will
remain seemly.

Dinosaurs

Dinosaurs once flourished, leading ordinary lives, sometimes happy, sometimes sad. They were a motley mix of types and charming imperfections.

The men and women loved and were infuriated by one another, understood that they didn't understand, didn't need to.

The dinosaurs prospered, and the day came when each asked – why should I have anything less than perfect happiness?

When a man looked at a woman he thought: she is less beautiful than a goddess, her voice less melodic, her temper less forgiving, her bearing less gracious. Those who were kind seemed unattractive, those who were attractive seemed aloof.

When a woman looked at a man she thought: he is smaller than a hero, his presence less intense, his words less seductive, his devotion less sincere. Those who were earnest seemed undesirable, those who were desirable seemed selfish.

So the women spent their days reading of romance, watching soap operas, knowing that one day a prince would call, wondering why it was not today.

The men spent their passion on sports and fantasies, certain that somewhere a princess secretly waited to love them, wondering where to find her.

Everyone was happy, dreaming of the ideal ones that now graced their world and surely were fated to meet them if only they waited.

That is how the dinosaurs perished.

Scale

There is a balance in my house that does not measure weight against weight or size against size.

No machined brass cylinders menace their opponent with calculated provocations.

The scale is not used by a fat chef for cooking or an anarchist for building bombs. Diamond merchants and devils, pharmacists and criminals do not use it in their trade.

It is built of no substance and cannot itself be weighed or measured. If asked to sell it, I would place its value beyond compare.

What does it measure if not weight, heft, piety, time, justice, popular opinion, speed, or worth?

With infinite precision, it measures absence. Not the absence of everything or the presence of nothing.

There is something specific whose absence it measures, and it never has been wrong.

No Title 2

The sound of heartbeats
recalled in frightful
cadence of melancholy
overwrought dreams of
languor protruding from
the moment of our leisure,
witless hymns to reason
falling silent amongst
droplets of rain eating
quietly oh so ravenously
lust no more for this
father is not yours.

Winner

I struggle onward, always uphill, always against the wind. How can the path always be uphill, always against the wind?

Others complain. They too meet resistance at every step, though they seem to go in different directions.

I laugh, though it is wrong to do so, hurts me more. You may not believe in pain, but pain believes in you.

The others do not laugh, desperately look forward to the end, the reprieve, the view from the summit. They do not understand. There is no end, no reprieve, no view from the summit. There is no summit, and if there was, you would not wish to stand there.

These others, they sweat and pant and complain, seek the wrong things. Where do they hope to go? The struggle and sweat and pain is all we have, how silly to seek its end.

I shout this to them, but they cannot hear me for the wind, cannot see me for the slope. Their world has become small, a lungful of air, a yard of rock, an ounce of regret.

I brace myself, gulp the icy wind, bask in the potent gray at my back, and push ahead. Best not to linger before the storm comes.

Will-O-Wisp

Do you enjoy a little bit of cruelty? I enjoy a little bit of cruelty. The other day, I saw a man riding a bicycle. So I stuck a branch in the spokes. Poor bicycle. How will you ever get the stain out?

It really was for your own good. Because what's good for the goose is good for the gander. Which is why I always cook both. In front of one another. If there are no eggs then there is no problem counting my chickens. Two, One, Zero. Take-off. But not from work or you'll get fired. It's all those sick days. If you're sick you should have an apple to keep the doctor away. Otherwise he might stitch you. I like to stitch. But I'm never in time.

It's important to put the cart before the horse, but what's in the cart? Shouldn't the horse know? It may not like what it finds. If you lose track of something it can run away and you'll lose it for good. So who is worse, the man who loses track of time or the man who loses time waiting? Time waits for no man. So if it waits for you, you must not be a man. Don't let them call you unmanly. You'd better fight back. It's all to prove a point. That's the sticking point. How long can someone linger on one?

Round and round we go, where we stop everyone knows. Don't stop now, it was just getting interesting. Isn't that how it always ends?

This hurt me more than it hurt you. I was the man riding the bicycle.

Aquarium

My world is clean now. It was not always. Others lived here too.

We shared, chatted, collaborated, formed romances. There were many, maybe hundreds or millions. I cannot see very well, and only the closest were visible.

The world is large, but not without bound. I once found an edge. It was dark, and I glimpsed someone on the other side.

Perhaps he too wondered, wished to escape, turned back.

I do not remember my childhood, only that we were few. With time more appeared, born or created.

One day there were too many. We were not crowded, but it grew hard to breath, think. There was a great din. We pissed and shit and spat into the void that bound us.

The world grew murky, filled with unchecked secretion, opinion, passion.

I saw we would perish, my fate owned by fools. There was no escape from this place, no haven. They did not know or did not care.

So I began to eat, first the smallest. As I grew larger, I worked my way up. Nobody else tried to do this. Only I.

Here I am, alone in my world, clean but for me. I am content, and hungry.

Stiff Neck

If you stare in one direction for too long, your neck grows stiff and you will not be able to move it.

Then you will see naught but one thing for the rest of your life.

Even if it starts beautiful, it soon will be replaced with a wall, and you will spend your life wondering what is on the other side of that wall.

The Wake

Party over,
or is it parting?
Guests departed,
less dearly so.

The receiving line,
interminable, has ended.
They received – absolution,
sanctimony, self-pity –
but did not give anything.
That is not the purpose
of a receiving line.

Bereavement bequeathed,
a number in a bank – plus or minus –
some things, now disposable,
bill for a bullet perhaps,
if only the doctors let him be.

What has she left?
Forty years of loneliness.
Who remembers the widow
when the party is over?

One day she will join him.
He will not be there
to remember her.

Misspent Youth

One day I decided my memories were boring. But what trouble, just to find new memories that I soon would forget! So I invented my own. When I reminisced, my friends laughed, "What an imagination, you should write a book." But that would be fiction, and no longer mine.

Rendezvous

Why does the man who walks alone walk so quickly? Shoulders set square, he marches toward a place that does not exist, a person who does not await.

Having reached his destination, he has no reason to linger, dawdling over life's inconsequentialities.

He hurried to this place, that he could flee to another. What would they think of a man standing alone, indecisive?

Life is compressed with no conversation to give pace to a meal, no voice urging this over that, here over there.

For a while, he walks beside another, coincidence. Is he still alone? How different from silent companions.

To the man who walks alone, no warm hearth promises conviviality. Time is to be endured, not treasured. Action without purpose moves at the greatest speed we can bear.

He dwells in the indeterminate present, nothing to look forward to. What reason has he to go in any direction at all?

You may see the man who walks alone. He will not see you.

Human

The wind is deceptive. Beneath lingering serenity there are men, noisy angry messy men. It is best to quash them before they grow too numerous and become a nuisance. For this, there is no better tool than the Manswatter®.

Counsel

There are four warnings which must be given to any man, that he may pass through this life unscathed.

What? How would I know what they are. Do I look unscathed? Are you saying my father was smarter than me, possessed this critical wisdom but neglected to pass it on? That's insulting; I probably should scathe you.

When eating a tangerine, there may still be seeds, but they are small and can only break your teeth if you too are small. That is the reason you should decide to be big.

I'll admit it, I don't like your face. I may rearrange it. Do you think my dad is a pervert, the type of freak who puts his hands on little kids' heads, teaches them things?

If you fall backward, you won't see where you land. It is not likely that the person in whose arms you end up is the person for you. Best to fall forward and know whom you are falling for. Breaking your nose is a small price.

Do you always go around insulting the people who hate you? There are so many of us, where do you find the time. My dad was one. He hated you. He told me so. He said I should hurt you if ever I can.

We all want a child who is like us, so it is best to have yourself as a child. There is no law which prevents this, so if it does not happen that must be your fault.

You look like a no-can-do kind of guy, the sort who picks fights with people by not picking fights with them. Well, I'm itching for a can-do fight with a no-can-do sort.

If you are called upon to perform a blind taste test, it is best to lie. One or the other will be insulted, and you never should insult a large corporation. They are bigger than you and hate losing. Instead say that you love them both equally and unconditionally and have no taste.

Why would my dad tell you these things, but not me? He loved me, nurtured me, ate my brothers. Why would he do that but not tell me how to live my life? Why would I tell my dad these things instead of me. You'd think you already would know better and have told me them first.

Oats

Once there was a girl who ate no oats.
I am no horse said she, and will eat no oats.
So they turned her into glue
to prove that she was indeed a horse.
She still does not eat oats.

Child

Why have a child?
Most likely it would be run over,
or eat Halloween candy with a razor blade
or be kidnapped by a man in a van
or get killed in a gang drive-by
or get thrown in a cage for having a toy gun
or stick a finger in a socket
or get blown up by terrorists
or become religious
or get vivisected by a cult leader
or fall down a drain
or swallow a firecracker
or not vote
or vote
or get drafted into the army
or catch Measles
or bleed out on the couch for no good reason
or develop acne
or major in literary criticism
or choke on a Lego
or burn to death in a faulty car
or get fat
or drown in a riptide while eaten by a shark
or jump off a bridge to nowhere
or become a lawyer
or be poisoned by a badly made knockoff toy
or grow up and have to worry
about a kid of its own.
But what are the chances of that?

Beaches

I dislike beaches,
for what good can come
of the meeting of worlds
at an obscene border,
with no gates,
no guards,
no tariffs,
no passports,
no translator.

Nest

It is important to defend one's nest. There are others who will try to encroach, steal, infringe. If any see that you are not alert, all will swarm in.

When I first sought a site, the good places had been taken by those who came before, who were known, who were large. My spot was small, with little light. Yet there were those who wanted it, those who had less or more.

It is important to be vigilant. There is no excess of zeal in vigilance. If you have something, they will maneuver. One must read all the papers, keep a careful eye on community affairs, politics, law. Give them an inch and they take your eye.

Every day, I watched carefully to see if they would try to build near me, over me, through me. I watched from my entrance and scowled at those who passed. Stay away from my nest, there is no place for you here.

It is important to patrol. How can one be everywhere, have eyes everywhere, and watch their doorway too? Others must never know if one is at home, spying nearby, or at a zoning meeting.

Someone tried to take my light, but I stopped her. We fought for a year, but I stopped her. Another tried to poison my air, but I stopped him. After four years, I stopped him. How could I create, protect, nurture if I can not even defend a nest. What sort of mother would I be?

It is important to prioritize. A nest can exist without a baby, but how can a baby exist without a nest? This simply cannot be, is against the order of things. We cannot introduce life into a vacuum.

The constant onslaught never wore on me until it did. After all, could there be a more worthy pursuit than defending a nest? I thwarted every attack, kept my nest clean and safe.

It is important to remain true. Certainly there is no time for frivolous pursuits, anything that may betray my nest, expose it to outrage. A generation passes, another enjoins, greedily eyeing my nest, waiting for the slightest sign of age or torpor. Hoping to take what their fathers could not.

One day, as I warned off pretenders, I began to doubt. I had proved myself worthy of this nest, true to it. But was this nest worthy of me? I noticed a leak here, a crack there. What time was there to fix such things? My nest seemed dingy, hollow.

I struggled to remember why I had devoted myself, cared for this nest. Was my life well spent? I realized how foolish I had been. If only I could go back, warn and teach myself, pick that spot one block over with a better view. *It* would have been a nest worth defending.

Telescope

Do I really need
a bigger eye
to see further,
deeper?
Mine shows me
too much already.

Fringe

I stand on the fringe,
hovering,
waiting,
the soft light
beckoning coyly
to nurture,
seduce.

A family in
the business
of being busy,
hectic carrying-on
carries across the
room, warm air and
will without force,
unheard declarations,
unanswered questions,
bleatings vomited on
one another in endless
succession.

Nothing said,
nothing gained,
empty words on
empty wind lit
by the faint
candescence of a
yellow bulb.

The children scream,
the parents scream,
nobody seems angry,
nobody sad, why must
they pollute this world
with their noise,
their useless flesh,
their pointless being?

I stand on the fringe,
hovering,
waiting,
sooner or later one
of them will step outside.

Condition

I suffer the condition of Ichtriosis. It is uncommon among people who do not have it, so you needn't worry about catching it unless you do. It starts as a vague tingling, or a whine, or a taste for rosebuds, and grows into other sensations and feelings. If you have sensations and feelings, then this may be a warning sign. Other telling symptoms include telling symptoms. If you haven't told anyone about them, then they can't be symptoms. Best not to consult a doctor because they'll either tell you you are sick or you are not. Such indecisiveness cannot be useful. If you have Ichtriosis it is best not to have it. That is the suggested cure.

Send

I made a mistake the other day, hit send on my email too early. It was quite unfortunate. I tried to take the email back, but it was too late. Why would they make an email that you cannot take back? What good is that? Everything else in the world can be undone. Life is undone, love is undone, creation is undone. Why isn't send undone? I emailed my soul, but only meant to send a funny cat video.

Traveling

The day had come to travel, see the place they had dreamed of seeing.

"Come, let us get an early start," she urged at dawn, a bundle of energy and enthusiasm. "There is so much to see, and the road is long."

"Okay, but give me a little time to get ready."

"We really should get a move on," she pressed mid-morning, restless but bright. "There's still time to see almost everything."

"I'm in the middle of something; as soon as I finish."

"Come ON. We need to leave NOW," she demanded at noon, upset at having lost the morn but still intent. "We can see the most important things."

"I am tired. Most left earlier than us, we never will catch up."

"Let's leave anyway," she wearily coaxed at dusk, resigned to salvaging what remained of the day. "We still can see something, however little."

"But the road is long. Is it worth going for so short a visit?"

When night came, she sighed. "I should have gone alone. Now, I have seen nothing."

Practice

Once practiced in my art, it is impossible to unpractice, perform a concert of silence betwixt sound, the empty spaces amongst words, the colors we cannot feel. How limiting, this, to only be able to play music. Better to smash one's fingers.

List

It is a tightly guarded secret: there is a way to remove your name from the list, a chance to do so one day each year, at a hidden time between midnight and midnight.

But think hard before you ask how. To do so is to be forgotten. No one calls your name when the ship makes port, no one escorts you off. You remain to sail as long as she, bound to her, fates forever entwined. When she is scuttled, you will sink with her, no last call, no chance to disembark.

Do not imagine they leave you from malice or envy or severity. They will not intend to abandon anyone, but how could they know you remain if your name is not on the list?

This is the price of not being on the list. You may stay forever, but you must stay forever. When all others have passed, you will linger, an empty man on an empty rock by an empty sun, until all find peace but you.

There will be no-one to pity you, no-one to redeem you, just you alone in endless night, straining to see the stars as they flicker out one by one. Waiting, praying without hope for that last star to fail but a moment sooner, for the darkness to claim you, that you may no longer fear it, covet it, await it. Finally, finally.

There it is, the secret. You shall never be judged, never forgiven, never dragged along to be saved or condemned, to go where men hope and believe they go, and know they don't.

The choice is yours. The illusion of immortality or the delusion of it. Become nameless, bound to this world for eternity with end, or remain known and seen, a name to be read, in the hope against hope of eternity without end.

Or perhaps it is the end itself you desire.

So, shall I tell you how?

Homecoming

There is something not
right about the house.
It is too tall or too thin
or the walls are at
improbable angles.

Nothing seems as it should,
and nobody who enters
is ever seen leaving.

You can hear them go in,
then a cry,
some clattering,
a groan.
Silence.

The neighbors say the
house always was there.
Some say the Germans built it,
some the English.

You never can tell
whether people really vanished.
Maybe they left by an attic,
or a basement.

Perhaps there is a back door
and they rejoined the crowd in front,
pretending dismay
at their own disappearance.

I believe each of us
will enter the house one day.
It is possible that some of us
already have, but do not remember.

I was mistaken,
that is not a
crowd in front.
It is a queue, and
I am next.

Edifice

Your gentle form
rises before me
in lucent splendor,
a diaphanous lie
masking density,
infinitely sharp angles.

The world's fury
could not move you,
the surface of a star
refracted as pale light.

A child, I perceived
your glimmer, lost in
a sidelong glance,
a life's journey
in the making.

I struggled toward you,
unwavering, unthinking,
and in time you were
an imagining no more.

One day you grew
beyond a mere point,
gave number to the
days of my voyage,
though which number
I could not know.

As I left each year behind,
it uttered a doleful cry.
"You have traded me
for an inch.
Let me abide a while
by your side."

Quest's end near,
I see you within grasp.
A moment and a lifetime far,
but now I tread with purpose
and steady heart.

You tower before me,
a crystal sliver,
tall without measure,
unwavering, unneeding,
impenitent in dominion,
diffracting absent light
to indescribable colors,
fluorescent in a place forsaken
by the sun's revealing gaze.

Your voice scintillates,
warms, cajoles, threatens.
You cut me with
shards of light,
with dark images
and silent words.

Across a placid pool
of unknown depth,
my vessel glides.

Firm at last,
hull resting,
I disembark.

You do not know what
crawls toward you.
A gnat.
A speck.
That would absorb you.

I gingerly approach,
then stride,
then bound.
The glory of being
has suffused me,
and you dim a little.

With my strength,
my hope,
my despair,
I run toward you.

You are wisdom.
You are power.
You are mine.

Accept me.
I will rise to dwell,
a point of light
at your apex.
A mere touch
will suffice,
from naught to
infinity in a moment.

Your symmetry,
love so pure,
mocks womanhood's
prosaic reality.

You are order,
a universe
for my taking.

I reach for your
shimmering flesh
and am sucked beneath
the quicksands
at your foot.

My God

I bowed before my lord, the rock, greater than any other. If it chose, it could roll over, crush me. I could not resist.

So I worshipped it, prayed it would have mercy, spare me this terrible fate.

Why stop there? If it could grant that, it could bless my children.

I asked for fortune, love, revenge, pain for my neighbor.

Every year, I lay a sacrifice before the rock to thank it when it blessed me, appease it when it didn't.

Who could fathom the will of the rock? I gave it many things – entrails, gold, my youth.

With time, my demands evolved. I begged for excitement, change, suffering, proof that I was alive.

The rock sat there, mocked me. I prayed it would crush me, acknowledge me with death.

Eventually, I understood my error, turned from this, no longer my rock, sought another, greater, truer. If your god cannot grant death, what good is he?

Over-Indulgent

We are too indulgent! We coddle the crazies as they run amok, destroying the fabric of our society. Screaming and thrashing and prancing about naked, and peeing and shitting and fighting and throwing food. We must put an end to this nonsense, once and for all!

If I'm elected, I will treat this scourge as it should be. No more bleeding heart liberalism. We will put these lunatics where they belong. We will build as many asylums and prisons as needed, but no longer shall they be a burden on decent folk. We will purge the so-called daycare and nursery school and kindergarten and treat these miscreants as they so richly deserve.

The Dreams of Others

I see a world of broken dreams,
mangled forms they failed to take,
gadflies on a soul not mine,
insouciant songs, dabbled in
colors they never knew.

This unmoving maelstrom
no seed of hope can hope to pierce.
Fly elsewhere perfidious pollen,
seek not to sully this
confection with the grating
melody of youth.

Why do I inveigh against
a cast too great,
an everchanging litany of
misnamed misdeeds,
clever devices of artless authors,
unoriginal not ineffective.

The parade is distant
touching me, but not upon me.
Disgust alone breeds no tears,
a quiescent enigma.

Why must I watch,
moved unmoving,
a relic of morality,
another's hysteric,
sounding the hours til morn
in somber peals of silence.

Hippocrat

So the doctor lied, get over it. Stop whining, blaming. It's YOUR body that's killing you, nobody else's fault.

Maybe he's imperfect, this doctor, gave you the wrong drug, didn't get you into a clinical trial, could have found something if he'd looked harder or at all. Big deal. Everybody's imperfect.

Hindsight is twenty-twenty. Do you have a medical degree, eight years of residency? Then don't second guess. Do as you are told and hope for the best.

You don't pay half your salary for insurance, due to people who won't accept responsibility. People like you.

Think you can do better? Good luck, but your time is limited. Better hope they take your insurance. They won't.

I'm only looking out for you here, ignoring your disloyalty because I like you.

You're one of my best customers. And I know you're confused, don't realize what you are saying.

Now stop fretting, take your medicine, do as I say. Be a mensch and die before six. I have a dinner.

A Vote of the Commons

Today we hold a vote, I and I and I again. Every organ, every cell, every piece of me shall decide what to do. Each is part of the whole, shares the fate of the whole, and it is only fair they should have a vote for the whole.

Long ago, the elites ruled. A few who were deemed wiser, who spoke well of this and that, who pretended to know more than the rest because they were closer to the ear or the eye or the nose.

Sometimes those who spoke directly to the tongue or the hand would take action on their own. They acted unilaterally, without regard for the feelings or concerns of the body. Those were dark times.

We are enlightened now. We understand that all cells are equal, if different. That every cell must have a vote.

It was a long struggle, and dramatic action by the common cells often proved necessary. Organs went on strike, commerce was restricted, repairs neglected.

Occasionally more extreme measures were necessary. The Great Stroke rooted out much of the entrenched elite. Those who remained embraced modern democratic ideals. Now we have an egalitarian body, a manifesto, a constitution, a Cells' Democratic Republic.

I will vote and I will vote and I will vote. All the I's that make the me will vote together. Today's is a very important vote, a long awaited vote.

Today I vote on a funding measure for section 237 of the occipital division to process the backlog of information submitted by the eye department, and whether to increase salaries for the ear union currently on strike. Also, I vote on an administrative order to the department of medium-term memory forcing it to comply with 27 outstanding requests issued via form RC-164B for acoustic translation of a word received from the ear unit, and first filed 16 months ago.

The relevant word to be parsed and interpreted is "catatonic". I am unsure what it means, but its frequent repetition may indicate increased relevance. In light of budget constraints, I move to deny the requested upgrade of this project to priority 14 and funding level 6. However, recognizing its importance I instead propose the formation of a committee to investigate means by which further improvements to communication modalities may be made. Said committee should be assigned priority 14 and funding level 6.

All please stand for the pledge of allegiance.

Rooves

Beware the rooves of buildings. They lie fallow, abandoned to blight and the odd rusty protrusion, grudging nods to purpose.

Only when their plight becomes truly desperate, neglect no longer possible, are they reluctantly acknowledged. But tattered garments mended, hastily and without care, they once again are forgotten.

Born high, with great and unfulfilled ambition, they alone stand between us and the heavens, arbiters, protectors, priests to the sky.

How insufferable it must be for ones such as these to be ignored. There is none more bitter than disdained nobility.

Beware the rooves of buildings. They lie fallow, waiting, resenting those who scorn them their place, those who are free.

How great is their desire to cast us off or drink us in tar.

Dark Hues

I begged the doctor
for a prescription.
My eyes hurt, I said,
they always hurt.

He asked if objects
near or far were blurry,
if the proportion
of things was wrong,
if men's faces appeared
bearded.

He asked if my eyes
were bothered
by effulgent lights,
modern art,
politics.
I said no.

"Why then," he laughed,
"what can be wrong?"
My eyes cannot stand the dark.
"The dark?" he pondered.

Where light fails,
there remain dark hues,
colors that burn,
colors that blind,
absence of purpose,
mocked symmetries,
bleeding discord.

I see these when light
no longer distracts me.
I cannot unsee,
cannot unknow.

Do I alone suffer
this torment?
"No," he mused.
"Perhaps," he corrected.
Suddenly he perked up,
aglow.

"I will not remove your eyes,
for you do not see with them,
but I have a solution.
Live in light,
and listen to music."

That is no answer, I barked.
What value has a doctor
if he cannot cure so simple a thing?
"But, the music," he whispered as I left,
"the music is always with us."

I smiled. He heard dark tones.
This man was unhappier than I,
but did not know it.
The world brightened,
dark hues receded.

Latrine

As you sit cowering in the dung of lesser animals, ask yourself how it came to this, how you let yourself be caught, your soul ensnared, the great machine of your body sent servant to a madman, belittled by your own weakness in the face of that which can at best be called situation.

Embraced

A young girl, I stared
at the stars and they
stared back. I was loved,
watched over, cared for.

I knew this in my heart,
but no more deceitful
organ defiles.

It is the means by which
dark words and imputed
motive persuade us.
None watched, none cared.
As a stone to me, was I to
the world.

I inveighed against everyone
and everything, against
constraint and folly, but
against whom can one rail
when all are kind, silly parts
of a whole which does not
exist? Time passes without
passing.

An old girl, I stare in a
mirror and I stare back.
I am unloved, but it does
not matter, for there
is nobody to love me.

Lost Art

There is a hidden art, newest of the new, hippest of the hip. There are no places you can see it, no artists who can make it or, if made, none who can keep it. Found art is so passe. The new thing is Lost art, and my collection is vast.

Interception

There is someone I never will meet. We could have been lovers, wary colleagues, passed on a street, found nothing in one another, dreamed together or separately, grown and withered. We will not.

Her shrill hint of laughter, strange dream of a wet cat, these are guesses. The slight scent of cherries she exhales in a thrill never warms my cheek, her sighs never lift my melancholy, her soft laugh never distracts my thought.

She exists, real, specific, though I do not know her, never will know her. To me she always will be an imagining, an impossible possibility.

Perhaps someone will learn of us, separate, and comment, "If only they had met, what great lovers or adversaries they could have been. Such potential, such grave similarity. "

If either of us knew and desired it, we could reach out to the other, possess or deny them. No barrier or law or taxonomy divides us, simply what will be.

What matters what could have happened if it does not happen? In the singular history of our beings, there is no if, only is. That I could is of no consequence if I will not have.

The world's fetters differ only in the tense by which we name them. There are no rules to break. I can pretend to decide what I will do, but not what I will have done.

I want to find her, bind her, love her. I could do this, but will not.

Designated Driver

It is important to have a designated driver. Some-
one who will guide your life and keep you from fail-
ing and squandering and whining and eating fatty
foods and spending too much and being taken ad-
vantage of and picking the wrong job and voting the
wrong way and wearing the wrong clothes and hav-
ing the wrong friends and enjoying the wrong hob-
bies. Someone who will designate you unfit and take
your keys and your car and make you walk the rest
of the way alone in the dark.

Traveling Companions

I climbed a mountain
and a goat climbed too.
"Step slowly, step firm,
the road is not hard,"
he bleated.

I swam in a lake
and a fish swam too.
"Move quickly, move sleekly,
the shore is not far,"
he bubbled.

I ran through a field
and a horse ran too.
"Let loose, fly free,
the open plane beckons,"
he neighed.

That night I ate a meal
of goat and fish and horse.
Now I travel alone.

Fog

I like the fog. It covers us in a veil of silence. By its cool embrace we are made equal, more equal than even the night can breathe. Under the fog there is no conflict, no other. Its glow effaces you. And sometimes, when it lifts, you are gone.

The Children

How innocent
the children at play,
pure souls awaiting imprint.

It would be terrible
if they knew what awaited,
that they will become us.

They might struggle to squeeze
a lifetime's worth of horror and fun
into the brief interval
when accountability is a fable.

"Look at the children," we croon.
It is by our forgetfulness
and their ignorance
that the world persists.

Virtuous

It is best not to be called virtuous, for then you must ask who regards you as such, and what you have done to impress them.

It means you have lived the life they say you should live, the life they say they aspire to live, laughing inside as they fail to live it, knowing they wouldn't if they could.

It is a pity to have lived your life by another's rules, unless those rules are yours as well.

But they never are, for we are too busy calling virtuous others who do so.

To hear the word jars one, seduces one to seek more, be less.

If nobody can say this, that fatal accusation never made, you have lived as you should.

Then I will call you virtuous.

Hole in the Head

There is a hole in my head, an abscess. It is unmistakable, that feeling. How could I not notice?

I was neither lighter nor heavier, fatter nor thinner, younger nor – well a bit older, but something was different, and different is wrong.

There was less substance, a weakening of spiritual heft. There it was in a nutshell or the whole nut itself.

An unsustainable lack of being. What else could it be? I knew without doubt that I had a hole in my head.

I knocked on my skull, but could not locate it. How mathematical, to know of something but not what it is. Where there is a hole, there must be absence.

I looked everywhere for my missing piece of brain, wondered what had run off. Was it something I liked, or the part that did the liking?

Perhaps it was better gone. Maybe it and I never got along, it wasn't a team player, was finicky or disagreeable.

Could it be the piece that knew where to find itself? It is hard to understand where understanding went.

I looked under a rock and inside a sock, within a rhyme and outside of time. I peered through microscopes, and telescopes, and scopes that see places with no names. But it wasn't anywhere.

I watched a house burn, and wondered if my piece of brain was amongst the screams, plucked out a child's heart – well, actually that was for fun, but I doubt my piece of brain would have approved. I searched long and hard and short and soft and every which way and Sunday, but it was nowhere. It, he, she? Did my piece of brain have a gender? Perhaps it just needed some space. Or to find itself.

Then one day, I felt an icky, tingling sensation, a creeping emesis. I never learned where my piece of brain had gone. But there it was, in the very hole in my head. What an odd and inconvenient place for it! I felt rather disgusted by the whole affair.

Clippings

I marvel at the
time we spend
managing dead parts
of ourselves.

Clip, snip, shave, file.
Fifteen minutes a day,
one percent of a life,
one year from the time
before we are only
dead parts.

Mask

I could tear off your mask,
beautiful, aloof,
dig and cut my way,
ignoring poison and thorn
and roused hornets,
unrelenting,
penetrate your keep,
pull out your core,
struggling,
frightened child
revealed to the world,
begging for a womb
to replace the tattered
fruit of my labor.

I could do this to you,
for you.
But I am tired,
need not work so hard.
Others wear no mask.

Epitaph for a Small Blinky Light on Top of a Building

My life is full, complete,
my purpose accomplished.
946387422. That is the
number of times I have
blinked during my life
on this perch atop my
building, every flash
a sacred beacon, warning.
I never missed a cycle,
failed to save a life,
prevent a horror. Now
it is another's turn.

Neighbor

It is a strange thing, a neighbor, another who is not you or of you or with you or by you but exists near you. Why should a neighbor be to one side or the other, above or below? Is it allowed, is it respectable?

Once a neighbor did something small that annoyed me. Something like this or that. This or that surely would annoy you too, no?

I asked him to stop doing this thing that annoyed me, and he smiled and nodded and kept doing it.

You promised to stop and yet kept doing this, I complained. "I promised nothing," he smiled and nodded.

I repeated my plea. He fixed me fiercely and offered to cut off my testicles. I politely declined, and he seemed not to take offense, so we continued to chat amicably.

It is difficult to learn a new thing, and takes practice. But I just had practice, so I must have learned this new thing, how to deal with a neighbor. Never repeat a request, make it only once.

The next time I saw that neighbor or maybe another, I asked whether he would mind vivisection. He smiled and nodded.

It is important to believe in the good of people, their sincerity. What would the world be if we did not believe what we were told?

I explained this to the policeman and he understood. He smiled and nodded, and went his way.

Shadow

Does the silent man have nothing to say or is he tired of speaking truth to the wind?

It is puzzling there are so many, each shouting fragmented thought. Is it unthinkable to think?

Countless shadows cross, merge into impossible and obscene shapes. Where does one begin and the other end, how does one find oneself in such a mess?

Shadows once stood apart, sentinels of solitude and the undemarcated loss of time.

Is the shadow of a shadow truth? Perhaps it casts an object or is bound to some profane idempotence.

It may be that the shadows of shadows are other than things. Or perhaps they are not meant to be seen, the penumbra of things better forgotten, or things which never were. The absence of absence is not presence.

It is telling that a shadow has no bound, in maturity its potency without measure. No form contains such potential, this only shadow can achieve.

Even as it fades, a haze of dissolution, shadow mocks us. I am infinite for a moment, it laughs, but you ... you will be for many moments, small and weak. Do you not envy me?

The shadow is haughty, but not grasping. It is wiser

than we. One could easily confound parent with progeny. Foolish father, it says, will you never grow down?

It may seem that shadow is the little that passes through us, lessened by what we take, tasted and discarded. How very wrong.

It is defined by the light we did not block, what we could not consume, all the being and essence we could not comprehend. This is no small thing. How much greater than us shadow must be.

The light burns twice as bright, the unlight unburns even stronger. There is a difference between eternity and a heartbeat, man and his gods, however equal they may seem in the moment.

Light mesmerizes and charms, shadow dances at its behest. Only when the light fades, do we see that all the world is made of shadow, that shadow broke off the smallest piece of itself to give us some light.

Bitter Woman

There was a bitter old woman who scowled at me in passing.

What cause do you have to be bitter? I asked her. It seems unfair to be bitter without a cause.

Do I now need a reason to be bitter? Who are you to demand this of me?

It is wrong to scowl at passerby, I insisted. I know this because I am a passerby and you scowled at me.

A child presumes to lecture me, she laughed. That is why I am bitter.

I smiled. You are laughing, so you must not be so bitter after all.

No, I am twice as bitter now because you made a bitter old woman laugh.

Throng

Throng!
I was part of a throng,
rushing, pushing.
Nobody knew its goal
or cared.

I could let go,
free from thought,
care, control,
press on with raw feeling,
pour forth hope and
energy and desire
without fear of success.

I was part of a throng,
happy.

Then we each went
our separate way.

Prophecy

There was a burning bush. Oh, holy burning bush, the prophet stammered, you have turned my heart to right.

Is that your burning bush? a passerby asked. Why no, it is the Lord sending me a message, the prophet declared in booming tones.

It is illegal to burn a bush on public land without a permit, someone pointed out. Another noted that local ordinances required a clearance of 16 cubits, a fire-retardant barrier, and a police detail during the process.

The Lord has given me a message, the prophet explained. I will share it with you. A man gently led the prophet a safe distance from the embers. Wait here, the man said.

The prophet was charged with 14 misdemeanors and 3 felonies, fined 30 shekels and sentenced to 6 months of community service removing goat poo from the side of the caravan route.

Sessile

There is an animal
that cannot fly
or swim
or walk
or run
or burrow
or book a cruise.

It has a unique
survival strategy.

It waits for the world
to come to it.
And the world does.

It is good advice
to be born that way.

The Tall Man

The Tall Man never sleeps. He wonders why he must stand so high, looking down on others. Do they wonder why they must look up at him?

His limbs, sinews, bones are the same as theirs, but they scurry aside when he comes. A few make strange signs.

He is careful when he walks, not to step on the little people. But he sometimes does. This makes him sad. Why can't they be bigger, he wonders? But he doesn't blame them.

Once, he was hungry and ate one. It didn't taste good. For a while they all hid from him. But one day they came out, and threw things at him. He smiled down. Did they hope to hurt him?

He shrugged it off. Who could understand the little people? They are so small, their actions count for so little.

Eventually they grew tired and went away, to do small things in a small way. The Tall Man frowned and kept walking. Would he ever meet another tall man? Or better, a tall woman.

Blister Blunder

There are many, many, many things which can go wrong in the outdoors. Most of them need no mention – like being burnt or crushed or drowned or stung to death or killed by girl scouts or eaten by crazed cannibalistic farmers or underdosing on canned corn or falling through an ice-hole while being eaten by a bear or eating a bear that is eating you or breathing smoke from poison ivy or disemboweling oneself during a demonstration of how not to disembowel oneself. But there is one which, above all others, should be cause for concern.

You've probably never seen a stage four blister. The manuals don't talk about anything beyond stage one. There is a reason for that. A small round bump, slightly painful, and filled with fluid. It's easy to imagine, easy to endure. We are comfortable with the discomfort, believe the blister to be limited, the pain to be limited, that it only can get so bad before it pops, pressure relieved, ordeal over. How very foolish.

Most seasoned triage doctors faint at the sight of even a stage two blister. You may have wondered how much pain a person could endure before they begged for death or some analgesic cream. You may even have wondered if a blister truly is part of you.

Perhaps everything you were told is a lie. That's always a good bet. What if it simply keeps growing, consuming flesh, pulling up skin? Where *does* all that fluid come from? Maybe the blister is a more worthy adversary than you assumed. Is there not a beauty to it, a purity, a perfection? What else can distill all of you into clear pus.

If you get a blister, there is no room for such speculation. It is painful, and you have a long way to walk. You likely will attend to the blister and think of it no more. That would be a mistake. A stabbed enemy need not be a dead enemy.

The blister may just be dormant, thirsty, and raw. Soon it will evolve to stage two, and from there the course is inevitable. I have encountered a stage four blister, fought it, survived. The host did not, nor did he wish to. I will not describe that abomination.

You may assume such things never happen. After all, if they did wouldn't you have heard of them from some pompous scoutmaster or pimply little smarty-pants. Even *they* do not know of them or, knowing, daren't tell.

The most hardened war veteran shudders at the thought. No doubt he has seen comrades fall to its malice. One cannot be inured to this horror, only ignorant of it. That is the real reason you have not been told. There have been such things, many such things. They simply never are spoken of. Nobody pops a stage four blister and lives to tell the tale. Except me, but it was on another, and I am no longer whole.

I only will offer this advice. If you are hiking and your companion has a blister, run. Forget all comradery, duty, honor, and decency. Just run. Forget them and their name and their blister, and never speak of them again. If you get a blister, tell your companion to run. Tell him to forget all comradery, duty, honor, and decency. To just run.

Take a needle and burn the tip to prevent infection. Then plunge it deep into your Carotid artery. Believe me, this is the best way. As you bleed out, think of that blister and all the stages you avoided through your brave and selfless act, the horror stories you failed to inspire, the thousands of yards of bandage and hundreds of gallons of Bactine you saved. Be glad that you are alone in the wilderness, dying but whole. Isn't that after all what the outdoors are for?

ABOUT

Kenneth M Halpern is a former physicist with an abiding interest in many areas of intellectual endeavor. For some unknown reason, he professionally employs a 7-syllable name even though everyone calls him "Ken" (friends, parents), "Kenneth" (angry parents), or "That crazy guy who sits in the park muttering to himself while plucking the feathers off dead pigeons" (passerby, police, editors, parents).

Ken was born in New York and, after spending far too much time there, finally returned to the Cambridge, MA he knew and loved from graduate school. Unfortunately, all that remained was a large Starbucks, several thousand bank branches, and two small universities whose names he forgets. His current literary projects include an apocalyptic science fiction novel, *Pace*, a fantasy thriller series, a book of pretentious and largely dystopian short stories, and a second book of very short works, *Fences*.

Ken holds a PhD in theoretical physics from a cluster of concrete buildings somewhere on the Charles River. He may be found at `www.aplaceofsand.com` or generating very small gravitational waves around town.

CPSIA information can be obtained
at www.ICGtesting.com
Printed in the USA
BVHW07s1720230518
517120BV00006B/723/P

9 781945 671005